Why can't I... sleep on a bed of bubbles?

and other questions about materials

Sally Hewitt

Belitha Press

First published in the UK in 2001 by
Belitha Press
A member of Chrysalis Books plc
64 Brewery Road, London N7 9NT

Text by Sally Hewitt

ISBN 1 84138 444 5

British Library Cataloguing in Publication Data
for this book is available from the British Library.

Series editor: Jean Coppendale
Designer: Jacqueline Palmer and Fanny Level
Picture researcher: Terry Forshaw and Ashley Brent
Consultant: Helen Walters

Printed in Hong Kong

10 9 8 7 6 5 4 3 2 1

Picture acknowledgements:
(T) = Top, (B) = Bottom, (L) = Left, (R) = Right, (B/G) = Background,
(C) = Centre

3 (TR), 15 (B) & 31 Chrysalis Images; 6 (B/G) & 7 inset (B/G) Chrysalis Images; 14-15 (B/G) © Digital Vision; 16 (B/G) © W. Wayne Lockwood/Corbis; 17 (B/G) & inset (B/G) © Ted Streshinsky/Corbis; 19 T (B/G) © Bryan & Cherry Alexander, B (B/G) © Michael Boys/Corbis; 24 (B/G) © Bill Ross/Corbis, inset © Wolfgang Kaehler/Corbis; 25 (B/G) Chrysalis Images, inset (B/G) © Michael Boys/Corbis.

All other photography Ray Moller.

Contents

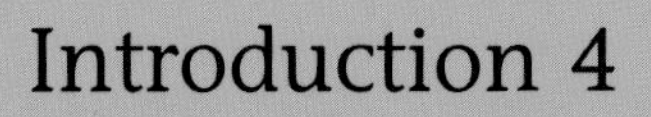

Introduction 4

Why can't I walk through walls? **6**

Why can't I squash all my toys into my bag? **8**

Why can't I stretch these shoes to fit me? **9**

Why do spilt drinks make such a mess? **10**

Why can't I mop up milk with a plastic bag? **11**

Why can't I see air? **12**

Why can't I fly on a paper plane? **14**

Why can't I wear summer clothes in winter? **16**

Why can't I swim on my tracksuit? **17**

Why can't I sleep on a bed of bubbles? **18**

Why can't I live in an igloo? **19**

Why does cake mixture change when it's baked? **20**

Why do candles disappear after they are lit? **21**

Why can't I cook with a plastic frying pan? **22**

Why isn't my doll soft and cuddly? **23**

Does blue wool come from blue sheep? **24**

Where does plastic grow? **25**

Why is it important to recycle rubbish? **26**

Material words **28**

Activities **30**

Notes for parents and teachers **31**

Index **32**

Introduction

What are you wearing?

Is your t-shirt made of cotton and are your shoes made of leather?

Have your clothes got **plastic** buttons or a metal zip?

We call the things that everything is made of **materials**.

Materials such as wood, wool or stone are all **natural materials**. They grow, come from animals or are found in the ground.

Other materials such as plastic are made in factories.

This book will show you how materials behave – how milk makes a mess when it spills, how plastic is not a good material for making saucepans and how bubbles don't make a good bed!

Why can't I walk through walls?

Because walls are **solid** and so are you.

If you tried to walk through a wall you would bump into it and hurt yourself.

A brick, a chair and a mug are all solid things.

Bricks make strong walls.

A mug holds your drink.

A chair supports you when you sit on it.

Why can't I squash all my toys into my bag?

Because your bag isn't big enough.

Your toys are solid things and you can't **squash** solid things to make them smaller.

You can try to pack your bag carefully to fit everything in, but you can't make your toys smaller by squashing them.

Why can't I stretch these shoes to fit me?

Because shoes aren't made of stretchy material.

If you grow out of your favourite shoes, you won't be able to **stretch** them, however hard you try.

Elastic is a stretchy material.

It will stretch when you pull it and snap back into **shape** when you let it go.

Why do spilt drinks make such a mess?

Because drinks are **liquid**.

Liquid doesn't have a shape of its own.

Milk needs a container such as a carton, a jug or a glass to hold it.

If milk spills out of its container, it will spread out and go everywhere!

Why can't I mop up milk with a plastic bag?

Because plastic won't soak up milk.

Plastic is **waterproof**, so it doesn't soak up any kind of liquid.

A paper towel or a dish cloth would soak up the milk very well.

Why can't I see air?

Because air is an invisible **gas** and you can't see invisible things.

Air is all around you.

You breathe air in and out of your lungs through your mouth and nose, so your breath is an invisible gas, too.

Even though you can't see air, you can feel it and see what it does to the things around you when it moves.

You know your breath is there when you blow out candles, blow up a balloon and feel hot breath on your hand.

Wind is moving air. You can see leaves shaking in the wind and feel wind blowing your hair.

Why can't I fly on a paper plane?

Because paper isn't strong enough to hold you up in the air.

A paper plane will fly a little way and then float through the air down to the ground.

A big passenger plane is made of strong, light material.

It flies because it has wings to lift it and a powerful engine to drive it through the air.

Why can't I wear summer clothes in winter?

Because you would soon get very cold.

Summer clothes are made of light materials like cotton that help to keep you cool on a hot day.

Winter clothes are made of thicker materials like wool that keep out the cold.

Why can't I swim in my tracksuit?

Because your tracksuit would soak up water.

A tracksuit will keep you warm on a cold day, but it won't keep you warm in the sea.

It would soon become heavy and full of cold water, and make swimming very difficult.

Why can't I sleep on a bed of bubbles?

Because the bubbles would pop and you would land on the floor!

Bubbles are beautiful balls full of air. They have a very thin, soapy skin.

Just one little touch breaks the skin and the air escapes with a pop!

Why can't I live in an igloo?

Because igloos are made of ice and will very soon **melt**.

Ice is solid water. Water freezes and becomes ice when it is very, very cold.

As soon as the weather gets warm, ice starts to melt and your igloo will become a puddle of water.

Why does cake mixture change when it's baked?

Because heat from the oven changes it.

The butter, sugar, eggs and flour in cake **mixture** all change when they are heated up.

Whatever you do to a baked cake, you will never be able to turn it back into sloppy cake mixture.

Why do candles disappear after they are lit?

Because the flame melts and burns the candle wax.

When you light the wick, heat from the flame melts some of the wax and it drips down the side of the candle.

Some of the wax becomes so hot that it burns away.

Why can't I cook with a plastic frying pan?

Because plastic will melt when it gets very hot.

Metal is a good material for a frying pan.

A metal saucepan heats up on the cooker and cooks the food inside it.

Heat from a cooker is not strong enough to melt metal.

Why isn't my doll soft and cuddly?

Because your doll is made of hard plastic.

A teddy bear is made of squashy materials which makes it soft and cuddly.

Plastic is a good material for making dolls, because it is strong and light and easy to wash.

Does blue wool come from blue sheep?

No. Sheep usually have white wool.

Sheep's wool is changed to make your jumper.

First the wool is **sheared** from the sheep. Then it is washed, dyed different colours and spun into **yarn**.

A ball of wool can be **woven** into cloth or knitted to make warm clothes.

Where does plastic grow?

Plastic doesn't grow, it is made.

Natural materials such as metal, wood, rubber and leather come from plants or animals or are dug up from the ground.

Natural materials can be changed in factories to make new materials such as plastic.

Why is it important to recycle rubbish?

Because a lot of our rubbish is made from materials that are being used up. One day these materials will run out.

Things made of paper, glass and some kinds of metal and plastic can all be **recycled**.

That means they can be used again.

If we throw them away with the rubbish they will be burnt or dug into deep pits.

Recycling helps to save precious materials.

Material words

gas Air around you is a gas you can't see and so is your breath. Gas moves around and has no shape of its own.

liquid Water, milk and oil are all different kinds of liquid. Liquid can be poured. It needs to be put into a container like a jug or a mug because it has no shape of its own.

materials Materials are what things are made of. Materials can be very different from each other. Some are soft, others are hard, some burn easily and others can be bent or twisted.

melt A solid melts when it is heated and turns into a liquid. Candle wax melts in the heat from the flame and ice melts in the sun.

mixture You make a mixture when you mix two or more things together. Cake mixture is made up of butter, sugar, eggs and flour.

natural materials Things that have not been made by people are natural. Wood, wool and stone are all kinds of natural material.

plastic Plastic is a kind of material that is made in a factory. It is not a natural material.

recycled Recycle means to use again. If we save our used paper and glass for example, they can be recycled. They are taken to a factory and made into new paper and glass.

shape All solid things have a shape. A book is a rectangle shape and an orange is a round shape.

sheared Sheep used to have their wool cut with big scissors called shears, so when they have their wool cut we say they have been sheared. Now sheep have their wool cut with electric clippers

solid A solid has its own shape. Solid things will keep their shape unless they are cut, squashed, heated or broken.

squash You can squash some solids like clay into different shapes by pushing them. Solids cannot be squashed to make them smaller.

stretch Some materials like elastic can be pulled and stretched to make them bigger. When you let them go, they spring back to their normal size.

waterproof Waterproof material does not soak up water. Water slides off it, so waterproof material is good for keeping things dry.

woven Cloth is woven by criss-crossing long threads of yarn on a frame called a loom.

yarn Yarn is made by spinning or twisting sheep's wool into long threads.

Activities

Here are some objects you might use every day. Match each one to the materials it could be made of. Ask yourself why the material is good for the object you match it to.

Objects

- saucepan
- coffee mug
- jumper
- shoes
- sunglasses
- pencil
- tablecloth
- chair
- balloon
- spoon

Materials

- glass
- clay
- wood
- leather
- cotton
- wool
- rubber
- metal

These words describe the way things feel. Can you find the opposites?

Notes for parents and teachers

Children know they can't sleep in a bed of bubbles but they may not know the reason why. Spend some time together thinking about the questions in this book and the possibilities they raise before reading the simple, factual answers. You may like to try out these activities with your child. They will reinforce what you have learned about materials and give you plenty to talk about.

Make some play dough

Mix together:
1 cup of flour
1 cup of water
1/2 cup of salt
1 teaspoon of oil
As you make the dough, discuss how flour and salt pour, even though they are not liquid. See how the dry ingredients change when you mix them with water and oil. Squash and mould the dough into different shapes. Bake the shapes and talk about how heating the dough changes it.

Sorting

Collect all kinds of small objects made of as many different materials as you can find. Talk about the properties of the materials – whether they are hard, soft, bendy, shiny and so on.
Sort the objects in different ways.
For example
1 The materials they are made of or from.
2 Shiny and not shiny.
3 Made and natural materials.
4 Hard and soft.

Paper

Find out about paper as a material. Collect different kinds of paper and talk about whether they soak up water, are shiny or rough - and so on. Use paints, pencils and felt tip pens to write and draw on the different papers. Fold, crumple and cut the paper to see how you can change its shape.

Index

air 12, 13, 14, 15, 18

animals 5

cotton 4, 16, 30

elastic 9, 29

factory 5, 25, 28

gas 12, 28

glass 27, 28, 30

ground 5, 25

heat 20, 21, 22, 28, 29

ice 19, 28

leather 4, 25, 30

liquid 10, 11, 28

materials 4, 5, 9, 15, 16, 22, 23, 26, 27 28, 29

melt 19, 21, 22, 28

metal 4, 22, 25, 27, 30

milk 5, 10, 11, 28

natural material 5, 25, 28

paper 14, 15, 27, 28

plastic 4, 5, 11, 22, 25, 27

recycle 26, 27, 28

rubber 25, 30

solid 7, 8, 29

stone 5, 28

water 17, 19

waterproof 11, 29

wood 5, 25, 28

wool 5, 16, 24, 28, 29, 30